LI]

Amanda Lauren

Ampersand Press | PRESS

LIMB & LIFE by Amanda Lauren

Published by Ampersand Press

www.ampersand-press.com

www.amandalaurenauthor.com

Copyright © 2022 Amanda Lauren

All rights reserved. No portion of this book may be reproduced in any form without permission from the publisher, except as permitted by U.S. copyright law. For permissions contact: amanda@ampersand-press.com

Cover by Kerri Resnick.

ISBN: 978-1-958172-00-1 (print)

Printed in U.S.A.

First Edition

Table of Contents

Foreword .... *vii*

I: Limb *1*

    Hands 2
    Strings 3
    Penny Platinum 6
    Purple Dragonflies 10
    Without Me 13
    Blackened Vessel 15
    The Weight of Water 18
    Wishbone 22
    Alphabet Shore 23
    Golden Leaves 25
    Haunted 27

II: & *33*

    19 & 9 35
    Honeysuckle & Vine 38
    Raspberries & Wine 41
    Black & White 45
    Tendon & Bone 49
    Iron & Wine 54
    Unit & Universe 60
    Limb & Life 64

III: Life *69*

    Can We Keep the Dog? 70
    Circling 73

How I Survived Him	74
Proof of Life	77
Fractal of Time	79
Shelter Sticks	80
Little Golden Girl	83
Centrifuge	89
Apple Seed	92
Acknowledgments	*93*
About the Author	*94*
About the Book	*95*

For Brooke

Foreword

Limb & Life

The process of making this collection has been an exploration into what it means to be alive. Without the vessel of my body, I could not have experienced the sensations of life that were vital to crafting these poems. The title is an inversion of the expression "to risk life and limb." Poetry is writing in its most concentrated form and therefore takes great risk in its attempt to find totality with its brevity.

The title is also a nod to a poetry book that I've owned for many years: *Unit & Universe* by I.L. Salomon. I bought the book at the Strand Bookstore in New York City when I was nineteen years old. The book had a gravity to me. It would not allow me to leave the store without it in my possession. That book felt as if it carried a message for me, and through writing my own, I've discovered what it was: I too am a poet. I would one day have my very own collection composed of units of growth and investigation and heartache. Somehow within all those units of humanness, I'd arrive upon a greater understanding of what it means to be a part of the universal—to risk limb and life for what keeps my heart beating.

Back to the sea,
where I felt you
and it and
all of it

I: Limb

Why not go out on a limb?

That's where the fruit is

—Mark Twain

Hands

Who paints the sky each night?
A hand like yours?

Blue veins shroud,
The way you moved through clouds.

Could I reach my fingers up to skim you?
Catch the whites of my nails on the moving winds,

Sails like halos,
Slipping right through me.

A kite, a balloon let loose,
A goodbye as silent as light.

But the ether comes alive,
Each night, evenings bright and palettes of life,

A new scene that restores an earth dweller's belief,
That up there exists a truth beyond my reach.

I submerge my eyes as I wonder when
The rains will open up, the painting incomplete—

The hand at work gave yours to mine,
But our fingers have torn a split in the sky.

Strings

He crossed my apartment in long strides.
I was there, on the other end of the rug,

The air had left my lungs.
See, when the words are gone and all that's left

Is a moment of truth,
I shrink. *You won't be able to see me.*

I was a thousand tingling strings,
My mind in every corner of the room.

He was like a ghost I could hardly get myself to see.
He could have been a fever dream.

Swift. Even quick.
He was in front of me. His mouth alive on mine.

I was halfway through saying
"I don't like kissing,"

When all the lies of my life
Pulled tight through my spine.

My words evaporated to the moment splitting back,
Catching up to rectify the feeling.

He froze like metal.
Stood straight and waited.

I was upright with no escape.
My milky backbone had to be brave.

Truth levitated
And words sank.

I liked kissing—*him*.
He caught my contradiction

By grabbing both sides of my neck.
In one sharp sounding chord he struck

Something in me,
Every cell hummed at once.

It was white hot fear. It was lightning, it was ease,
My erratic heartbeat steadied.

From every corner of the room,
I came back to my body.

Instantly he was human too.
Four long limbs and a knowing grin.

I'd stumbled upon a lost key.
He made me pure electricity.

The wires of me, the fibers of me, the risk in me,
Was finally broken free.

— Sinner, sinner, serpentine
You are cinnamon

Penny Platinum

You are cinnamon.
Chrysanthemum,
Orange plum.

You beat on the concave
Love of my breast,
Like a summer drum.

You call on the hummingbirds,
Nectar, and seed—ylang-ylang,
A strong steady breeze.

With you I could twirl once more,
In daybreak of amethyst skies,
Inhaling fumes of cherry cough lies.

You could make me bloom with honey thyme,
Steeped in another woman's nursery rhyme,
Her efforts from yesteryears.

Or you could drop me like a dime,
For you could pick any penny you please,
Deceivingly shiny.

Eye-catching from the oxidized
Ruins of long gone polish,
Laid to burial,

Beside snapped rose stems,
Winter's mulch—
Reciprocal.

I hint to you now, my silver shall fade,
It'll coil, grow ablaze,
Like a live wire tuned up with forgotten rage.

I'll be copper that clings,
But don't go.
Our fingers will survive,

Intertwined,
By the committed night light,
Sipping one true tea with ease—our love sustaining.

But there's the stanza break,
The heaven's sake,
The god-mistaken fate of it all.

Your hunger,
Your greed—
That wondrous depravity.

Scoop from me my taboo.
Dunk me in the wishing well.
I'll be bathed in caveats.

For you I'll spiral,
Pirouette,
Confess . . .

Gut me clean,
Like the downstream.
Strip me from the church boys' choir.

Breathe me new.
Consume me full.
For you, I promise not to tire.

You have me strung out on a trapeze,
Toeing the line,
Sensation overdrive.

Sinner, sinner,
Serpentine.
You are cinnamon.

3/22/21

Penny Platinum

You are cinnamon, chrysanthemum, orange plum

You beat the concave of my chest like a summer drum — calling on the hummingbirds, nectar and seed — ylang ylang, a strong steady breeze

With you I could twirl once more in the daybreak of

Purple Dragonflies

Indigo flowers bloom from lilac nights.
Remove my bathing suit.

Love me new
In our infinity pool.

Smooth my hair back with your hand,
Until my eyes gleam at you wide.

The water will soothe the rifts
That walking on earth brings.

These pupils expand in moonlight.
Dial into me; sink into me—

Water's buoyancy.
We're floating.

When I was a child, there were dragonflies.
They flew above the pebbled pool.

I watched them connect—dragonfly sex,
And I knew that humans made a mess.

The dragonflies didn't test.
They didn't clip each other's wings

But flew in union.
They didn't have to learn to be that way.

Their wings were tissue—spindles and veins.
Their delicacy on display.

They never feared hurting each other,
Even for being naturally weak.

They were fierce as a pair.
Flew with the strength of a fleet.

My human heart ached,
To fly that way.

Above the swimming pool,
Shimmering blue.

Even at nine, I desired a simpler life.
To not be twisted like the people I lived with inside.

Now, my wings are strapped.
On my back.

I'm in the deep end,
Wondering how I got here,

Wondering how it got so messy,
Wondering why I still cry over the people inside.

I hadn't seen the dragonflies in some time.
So, I ventured indoors.

Spice cabinet of oregano,
Teach me how to play piano.

I want to use my fingers the way humans do.
Chop veggies for a frying pan,

Nap with you under a cooling fan,
Fly with you inside.

It shouldn't be scary,
But it's a natural habitat of disaster,

Where it all burned in the beginning,
Why I hide in the pool.

French doors that locked the monsters inside.
It was hard to remember why dinner hurt

When I watched the purple dragonflies.
They drank from the birds-of-paradise.

They slipped into the palm trees
When the night came.

I wondered how they cuddled—
Wings layered like origami paper.

Without Me

I wake, but I fear being seen.
Barricade me in blankets.
Linens of—*don't go yet?*

I wish not to rise,
Let my bones take your weight instead.
Hold me down and maybe I'll feel revived.

This ever-returning feeling
Keeps on stealing—
My time, my cheer, and my promised years.

I know no freedom from this tiredness.
I can't peel the curtains
Or my morning eyelids.

The sun might mock me.
Everything burning on without me:
The day, the children's parade, the ecstasy.

Can you pull me from my pillowcase chains?
Hang me with wooden clothespins,
My shoulders strung out with last night's sheets,

So the wind can blow through me—dry me clean?
Or will you look away when you see *it* in my eyes?
Don't be terrified.

Grease on the heat

Blackened Vessel

I'm padded with armor—steel of indifference.
No voyager will raid this ship, break open the vault
Where I've shoved all my tenderness.

I cut through the fog.
The coveted night where I let myself bleed.
My writer's tongue rung.

The possession in my veins.
Pins and needles in my brain.
Everything is more clear when I can't see a thing.

The darkness greets me.
I can hide in the folds of silence.
A beautiful abyss of my accustomed sadness.

A private escape that never sees the light of day.
By the break of dawn,
I've drowned my darlings.

I take no risks with my heart—
The waves, the stakes—both are too high.
My blackened vessel is quiet in the sunlight.

Four chambers with no flow.
No circulation.
The pump of blood and lust and love—

All of it becomes compartmentalizations.
Separations cut from any resurrection.
A fundamental disconnection.

And suddenly it becomes clear
That I've been guided by the devil in disguise:
My own mind.

Perched in my skull,
Steering the ship,
Throwing gasoline on every insecurity.

Like grease on heat.
Strangling the beat
Below my ribbed bones.

Shutting the valves until my voice fell devastatingly
Hollow and unable to grow.
I'm so afraid that I'll never be free

From my own limiting beliefs.
I've gone and locked myself in my own purgatory.
Are we ships passing in the night on a cold,

Endless sea?
All this logic-based sovereignty.
Death of connectivity?

Can I repair my pathways?
Grow new arteries? Do I dare
Release these burned and buried parts of me?

I feel so bruised and I don't know who I'm talking to.

(grief)

The Weight of Water

I was blindly nineteen. My body unbroken. My mind not yet lost. I had goals with proclaimed purpose. A girl who thought she'd be victorious. A gladiator against men. A girl who hated children. I had such misguided contempt for the tears that would gush from my eyes, the femininity between my thighs. I locked my desire in a box. Muzzled my sensuality mute. In a world of rape, I tried to survive by having nothing to take. I thought I could defeat it all if I could stand tall. A giant against my fears. I reformed the rawness of myself. I grew calloused by ambition. I began to cut out slivers of my soul. I buckled those pieces of me into a lifeboat, banishing them from my ship, bidding goodbye, bit by bit. I pushed the fiercest parts of me out to a woman eating sea. I swore I'd have no love for my babies or my girlhood dreams.

All my ideas of *brave* were illusions like a cave. My back was to everything I was missing, depriving, starving. My eyes only focused on men's teachings. The shadow showed the formula that left you professional but not *unfuckable*. Tip the scales with one misplaced hair and they'll blow out their torch. The game is how good you can maneuver through eggshells of masculine egos all while being ready to fall to your knees. *Such a professional.* Something began to pull at me. That little girl who had different dreams. She spoke to me, "You forgot me." And then she whispered, "Don't you see?" She tapped on my back with urgency. I turned around to her bright-green eyes—joy reflected at me. "I'll show you where you need to go."

We arrived at the beach. I told her the sea hadn't been kind to me. I didn't want to face those abandoned parts of me. I dropped her hand to go back, but in a child's delicate screech, she called after me. She said it was time I learned what it meant to be brave. I turned back with reluctancy. She held the ocean mist in the globe between her hands. "Don't you feel that?" I didn't feel. I told her she was crazy—she was holding nothing. She looked away. Her bare feet almost foreign to me. "Who have you become?" She sighed.

Then I caved at the knees. There was so much lost that all washed over me at once. Those long lost bits slammed back from where they'd laid dormant on the ocean floor. They wept when they were met with this shell on the shore. I cursed the sun for my hurting—the purging. *There are no good men. There are no free women. There is no value in my art. There is no safety in sex.* The sickness was endless. All of it pouring from my stomach. The tide lashed out and grabbed my empty body. The ocean swallowed.

Then I awoke all washed up. Seaweed was stuck in the cutting edge of my teeth. I was thirsty. The child in me was gone. I was met by the woman who was angry. She said, "When did you decide we don't deserve to feel the ocean? My girl, you've lost your pearl. This world isn't your oyster. There is nothing to conquer. You've been so busy fighting tides that you let all the water in you die. Where are those tears that gush so sparkly, the glitter of seaweed, the throb between your thighs? Where are your lips that should be kissed? Your fingers need to be licked. You have hips of marble and breasts of butter. You were not made to please, and you were certainly not made to hide."

She was naked in front of me. She was Aphrodite. She threw away all shame. She commanded, "Touch me." The sea's great orchestration lulled into smooth melody. The water kissing in a low hiss. I saw then that she forgave me. She stepped into me. Within the shell of my ear I heard, "I am not weakness; I am Empress."

Baltic Sea
Come away with me.
You are my muse,
my contemporary,
you are a
masterpiece

Wishbone

Your lips—I wanted during Christmas.

Stockings falling at your feet.
My knees under the whisper of your teeth.

But like a wishbone torn in two—
You struck me with seconds

To be unraveled for a lifetime.
You were clock hands unkind.

Cupped the apple of my cheek
And stole the better side of me.

Half of my locket.
My lung in your pocket.

Blow me some breath.
Compressions to the bone.

The cold shimmer of my wish.
For finger imprint.

To be breathalyzed
Through the passage of this slow time.

Your lips miss the stroke of midnight.

Alphabet Shore

I scribe your name through sand.
Like ink of a snail trail.
Flocking feet pass by me.
I use twigs of technique.

My feelings bleak as I fill back
The grains you took from my teeth—
Hollow space of bittersweet.
Your aftertaste lingering.

Alphabet shore.
Look at how my truth pours;
From driftwood that broke like me,
Now I'm tumbleweed.

You disoriented me.
My compass no longer points
To the sea,
But my words remain buried on the beach.

There were so many
things I wanted to
ask you but you
wouldn't let me
within reach

I wanted to
know what you
thought about
everything

Golden Leaves

I can remember everything—
And nothing,
From that first night,
When your lips found mine.

I recognized you like a snap,
Like a tremble in my knees,
Like a bruise wading in the deep.
You drew back a forgotten part of me.

You were cornea swirls of *I've known you before* . . .
Heat shot down through my feet,
Like woven roots of a tree,
Golden leaves reaching to the ceiling.

I knew you bled like me.
We were the same shade of whatever beats beneath.
Beaten golden blue.
We were broken in two.

Cornea swirls of
"I've known you
before."

Haunted

I can still feel you at the back of my throat.
Crowded in my mouth next to my question:
Do you know that I've fallen?

You were a floral button-down coming undone,
Wine, and apathy—
That's all you offered me.

But my body knew you like a memory, and despite
Every flaw, you were raw. Some sort of kismet
And I craved all your earthly flesh.

You haunt me, you know. In the quiet of the night
When it's only me and the sheets.
I think of that time you hit me.

"I like to be rough, but it's all in good fun."
Your ice eyes dazzled as you confessed it and
I told you I agreed.

But then your hand slapped my face,
And it was like you swiped away my identity.
Beneath you I could hardly breathe.

You touched me like I was sturdy.
And God help me, it was holy,
But I was breaking in your hands.

Once in the middle of me being on my knees,
You asked me—
"What do you want?"

And if I had been half as honest
As I was in love with you,
Maybe we would've had a chance.

But every time you silenced my deepening feelings
With the brunt of your body,
I knew you couldn't swallow the answer.

With every dividing stroke
You wordlessly spoke—
"Why would you love me?"

And with every kiss at the altar of your hip,
I confessed—
I don't know.

I hope your ribs ache
For how you didn't cherish me.
I was never meant to be temporary.

Part of me hopes you are a man deprived of peace,
That when you lie alone at night you only hear
Echoes of: "You lost me."

And even though I must be gone
From your life,
For all the realest of reasons,

In the still of the night,
I think of a world where we could love again:
How you'd find me and never release us.

How you'd touch me
Like your survival depends on it.
You'd canvas my whole body with your hands,

Memorize it like it's yours
Before you mark it burning red.
Touch me so tender

That it could be mistaken for a whisper.
Kiss my neck, navel, and knees.
I'd want to be at your mercy,

But I'd have to know you love me completely
Before you're rough with me.
Then I'd want you to abandon fragility.

Open me fully. I'd want your fingers curled deep,
Your hold in and around me—
Abrupt and firm.

Pull me swift to the edge,
Kneel as your shoulders support me.
Your head between my knees—*lick me.*

Redemptive,
That's how your strokes should hit
When you finally enter me.

It should feel like you're
Begging with your apology.
"Darling, I'm sorry."

But then I'm jolted from this world.
I can't keep reliving your
Phantom apology.

I've written it in my mind,
All the things my heart needed to hear,
But it's only brought more drought to my ears.

I make myself remember—your cold eyes,
How they shined like a butcher's knife,
How you unremorsefully carved this mark

Into my life. I make myself see—
The apathy, the wine,
The floral button-down coming undone.

You play back in a rewind.
You're so terrible but you're true.
I can't seem to undo how I felt about you.

Because in the plight of the night
All I feel is belief
That you were exactly who I was meant to meet.

You're still at the back of my throat.
Crowded in my mouth next to my question:
Do you know how badly I'm hurt?

I wish
you'd bridge
our sea and
speak to me.

# II: &

*It's so eternal. As long as there are people,
they can remember words and combinations
of words. Nothing else can survive a holocaust,
but poetry and songs.*
—Jim Morrison

I make the choice to take the gamble with my heart, because

19 & 9

"I call it 19 & 9 because in New York City
My apartment was on the corner of
West 19th Street and 9th Avenue."

I want to know you—
The Nordic language you speak,
And your near-decade of experiences ahead of me,

You make the blood in my ears thrum
As I run to keep up, so afraid of an eclipsing sun,
Like you'll set on me.

Amber buzz and head rush.
Slip away and fade like Mexican beer bubbles,
Or burn the way that German gin stings.

See, you keep giving me all these tastes
I haven't thirsted for before.
Barley hops,

And all these words
That I never thought could ring to my liking—
"Babe" and "Darling."

See, you tell me these snippets,
Stories like 19 & 9, and I'm blind
And tied for the next direction,

To let you have some glimmer of me,
Some connection.
But my tongue runs dry,

Like golden wheat.
I can't compete.
I search for words you haven't heard before,

Some far away and to add,
But my mind spins
And then my limbs grow limp

And my hands close in.
And, and, and—
Ampersand.

lay me open,

let it (dissolve)

Honeysuckle & Vine

Brush that scent on my pulse point.
Wind my wrists with the garden's vine.

Under your linen canopy,
Shading our publicly indecent heat.

I'm sprawled out.
Legs raised to summer's day.

From the corner of your sky-bright eyes
I want you to watch me play.

Do you see that I'm glowing for you?
Basking in honey and rays.

Breezy, easy,
Tangerine, sanguine.

I look up above.
Reveling in the sun,

Dripping from coming
So shamelessly undone,

Like a fallen yellow dress
Left as a tent for the garden friends,

Already stained with white grape wine.
A perfect bed for growing dandelions,

The softest of vines.
I lay in nature for you.

Meadows of baby's breath,
And honeysuckle on sheets.

Don't be a voyeur, silly boy.
Come and squeeze me.

Citrus kiss—
Nectar on your fingertips.

sex in
the kitchen,
flip me,
lips slipping
on a silver
spoon,

Raspberries & Wine

I'm trying to be hungry again.
To feel something like contentment.
To stand on my toes again.
It's been dark for eight days straight.
My belly begged to glow again.
I craved the syllables of my own name—
To taste the three *A*s.
I'm a soft red filled with rose petals
And garden radishes.
I'm earthy and delicate, like thinned blood.
I've been living on crumbs.
I needed you to remind me
Of the way that my heart can beat.
The way that I'm alive, fleshy,
And full of human heat.
I bought you raspberries.
I wanted to see the pink on your lips,
Gift you your favorite fruit,
And ask you if I could keep you.
The wine was for me.
I wanted the full body of it against my tastebuds.
I wanted it to reach down deep
Into me and untwist me. I wanted
Coconut whipped cream and strawberries.

I wanted you to consume me. Make a meal
Out of me, but I've starved this body.
I must eat for me, to know survival
When I'm on empty. To find fuel in forest fires,
To not be burned by your cruelty.
I want tables—tables full of celebration,
A cornucopia of what you mean to me.
I want that harvest returned; winters survived
With me. I'll celebrate my own coronation.
Blood and bread of loving this body.
I live in this skin. It's harbored me for
Years without rain; it deserves water again.
Latin for worthy of love. Blue iris, tulips, sunflowers
And the most orange of gourds. I believe
I have seasons of more: A home of my own
Creation, where fawns feast on flowers.
A lover who's fed from reaping what they sowed.
An overflowing source for which I'll mirror
Like a flood. The purple pulse in the plum
Of my heart will bloom for someone new,
And I'll only distantly remember you.

7/6/21

Raspberries and Wine

I bought raspberries because I wanted to see the color against your lips, offer you your favorite fruit and ask you if I could keep you, an offering to my fears. The wine was for me.

play me like
piano keys,
press into me.

Black & White

You had a potency that spoke to me.
You pressed into me.
Played me like piano keys.

I let you build me,
Fashion a house of cards so carefully.
But you had no intention to keep me.

It was a faulty foundation of deceit.
I fell like a row of delicate dominoes,
Folding in so lovely.

The explosion a distant melody.
You offer me no remedy.
I knew you were a silo anyway.

You rolled your dice with me,
Only showed me few sides.
You should have bet on me,

Instead of moving me like a chess piece.
I kept landing on your locked-up boxes—
Our hearts in crosses.

I needed to know what I was missing,
Puzzled by all your inconsistencies.
I had too many blanks to breathe,

Feeling like a weight could come
Crashing down on me.
But I saw good in you, a full luminous moon.

I know now, nothing about you was black and white,
There was no magic eight to show me the way.
You were a spectrum of gray.

of cards ~~placed~~
~~cards,~~ so carefully,
~~a foundation~~
~~of half truths.~~
~~lies you told me~~

I fell like a
row of delicate
dominoes,
folding in so
lovely;

Silo

Tendon & Bone

I think about fine lines.
The construction nails dragged through your skin

From building homes for the pigs;
They scratched you for your decency.

An espresso machine that had it out for you,
A scar on your arm, like a pond where liability lies.

The inevitable remnants
Of moving through being alive.

A cyst on your side.
You packed the wound with gauze yourself because

You don't believe in a day off,
And at what cost?

The first time I kissed you:
Reflective eyes and our stacked thighs.

I touched your face,
Cheekbone, and nose.

You had a mark like mine,
But you told me it was fool's gold,

That it would scab away in a matter of days.
I kept kissing you anyway.

I asked you if the patch on your
Bronze shoulder was a Band-Aid,

Because I've never used nicotine.
My kitten gave you a scratch that made you bleed.

Fourteen miles in one day to stay in shape.
To chase away, far away, like eyes lost in space,

The jitters in your veins.
It's how your vacant gaze torments me.

The thought of your bodily injury.
Knowing you've been swallowed up.

Dark crescents cradle blue,
You swallowtail butterfly, you.

Gaunt eyes,
The cost for flying high.

When you don't know where you're going to
Sleep at night, will land like a crashed kite,

Wrapped around a tree with metal and leaves.
Broken ribs are the beginning of wings.

All this risk to reach Nirvana?
To be another Cobain?

I promise you there is no glory in that hall of fame.
You almost died on an airplane.

Taking pill after pill to escape,
But what you're running from is

Staring you blank in the face.
I want to throw my bones in front of yours,

To keep you away from an oncoming train.
My own body aches from absorbing your pain.

Don't you see that you're selling your soul
One finger at a time,

Like the girl in the art print that hangs on your wall.
Her vertebrae are being auctioned.

It's a caution, that once it begins it's a conveyor belt,
A slippery slope of broken skis,

Where you awake to no woman,
Only the wind carried away on a breeze.

Stop selling your fingers.
Give your pinky to me,

So, I can attach it back,
Sew tendon to bone,

Kiss it new, like your mother would do.
How she would cry if you told her the truth.

Your body is her baby.
Your body is begging.

You are only tendon and bone,
You've poisoned your limbs

With too much to hold.
I pray that you get to grow old.

Hearts and courage
ripped apart

Iron & Wine

A series of true things: The morning before I met you, I had a panic attack in my office's parking lot/ My lungs pumped like an accordion/ The sobs drummed out of me in sync with the March drizzles/ I was crying because my life had become an unrecognizable speck in my father's storm of a world/ I was working for his company/ Every day he occupied another corner of me/ In this fog, I was forgetting—who I wanted to be/ After the panic attack, I called out of my job and I drove to the beach/ I wrote a poem about a dog/

I almost never met you/ I came a heartbeat's leap close to canceling/ I'd opened my phone to send the message, but you'd already sent me a video of your face, saying how excited you were for the date, that swayed me the other way/ The persistent rain landed you in my apartment/ You brought me a Swedish soft drink made of hops and malt/ I was worried you were trying to poison me/ You seemed as ungrounded as me, as if you wouldn't have been able to recall how you'd arrived in this moment/ There was a flightiness in the air, like we both didn't want to be there/

Then you asked me if I'd ever seen a kiwi bird/ You said they were "flightless"/ When the word lifted off your thin lips, heavy with your accent, I was reminded of a song that I love: "Flightless Bird, American Mouth" by Iron & Wine/ I played the song for you/ You had a strange look come across your face/ "What?" I'd asked/ You said you thought it was going to be a joke, but "that was beautiful"/ The air in the room shifted/ In the collision of you kissing me, I could see beyond the fog/ Beams shone straight through the course of my life, and for the taste of a second, I could see clearly who I was meant to be/

On my patio you looked down at me/ You shook your head softly, your eyes closing like full moons, as if you were repenting under the night sky/ You shook your head like you couldn't decide between laughs or cries, as if my standing before you was a tragicomedy/ You shook your head like you hadn't meant for this to be what it was—*something*/ It was something/

You were a musician—the kind of musician that doesn't have another job/ I googled your name on my work computer the next day/ Then I closed out the tab so no one would know/ You were my secret as much as I was yours/ You were sending me videos of beagles you'd rescued from a testing lab/ You were so many things all at once, this complicated painting taking shape/ I started to feel the fingers of my soul pulling at my body's seems/ I ran to the bathroom, locked myself in the stall, turned my chin up to the ceiling/ I was in blackness when I asked—*Who am I? What do I do?* The blackness answered back—*You write, you write/*

You warned me, that you'd "lived a life," over the dinner you'd cooked for me/ I asked if you'd ever cheated/ You said you'd only ever been on the receiving end/ Some Canadian actress had messed you up badly/ I knew you one week but I would have kicked in her teeth if given the chance/ I listened to every song in your discography, trying to translate your past/ When you asked about my writing, I told you none of it's about any one thing/ Meaning, none of it is about you/ I was lying/

Monkey 47 is your favorite gin/ You got a bottle for your thirtieth birthday/ 47 is my lucky number/ When we went to the bar we ordered two gin and tonics/ I've never been comfortable in a bar, I always say "I'll have the same" as whoever I'm with/ You nodded to the bartender like he was a friend/ I look out for those sorts of things because my father was a drinker/ The bartender knew you/ My mother told my sister and me to never fall in love with an addict/ I half internalized her advice because my mother was never really in love with my father/ I was in love with you/

In April we walked from your house to a little coffee spot/ I was so trapped in my mind that bits of me were blowing away and catching on the shrubbery/ I have anxiety/ When we sat, you told me your sister and her partner were trying for a baby/ I asked if you were excited to be an uncle and you looked at me like I'd offended you/ You said "not really, but maybe when he's fourteen I'll give him drugs"/ It reminded me of how when you were fourteen your father had left you in the airport when he boarded the flight without you/

You said being in your thirties without children is like being in your twenties but with money/ I was only twenty-two and every incapable part of me wanted to be a mother someday/ I'm afraid I might not be fit to raise a baby/ I have depression and anxiety/ I want to name my daughter Felicity/ The name means *happy*/

After coffee you told me there was something you wanted to show me/ You tried to hold my hand on the way there/ We arrived at a lot that was for sale/ It had an abandoned house with a purple door/ You talked about *laying roots*/ You picked me up so I could look through the window/ I've always worried about what I weigh/ I asked if you wanted to stay in San Diego/ You said "I don't know what I want, maybe I just want a tiny house and not to have any roots"/ You retracted it all back just as I had with my hand/

I saw how the wine swayed like a jump rope, a few gulps below the surface of the cup/ You couldn't last a twenty-minute drive without it in the holder beside you, like you were tethered to it/ Over dinner you talked about your father's house in Sweden/ You said you hoped to inherit it one day/ I said "I thought you wanted a tiny house"/ You said, "I only want it so I can sell it"/

Your wife travels in a van with another man/ If you wanted a tiny house, you could have gone with her instead/ You told me your last relationship ended six months ago/ You said "I want you to know there is nothing between us anymore," as if there wasn't a marriage license *between* your names/ She's from New Zealand/ When I found out I was flightless/ There's still a picture on your Instagram where you're wearing the ring/ You told me how you married her after three months/ It was "a little crazy"/ There wasn't a wedding, only a small party in your father's backyard/ As a child of divorce, I've never dreamed of being somebody's *wife*, but the little girl in me has always envisioned herself as a bride/

The next time you talked to me you said drinking was almost a problem/ You said, "I remember what you told me about your dad"/ You said, "Thank you for even talking to me"/ You told me you thought about dying/ You said if it ever all gets to be too much, there's a gun store around the corner/ I've battled with my own brain enough to know when someone doesn't want to be alive/ I'm not religious in the ordinary sense, but I pray each day that your body still breathes/ I owe a bit of my own survival to you/ I quit my job because you told me doing nothing is sometimes worse than the consequences of doing something/ I never got to tell you how much you helped me/ I moved

Across the country/ I needed steel town clouds and the mouth of the sound/ After the move, I'd call my mother crying, almost nightly/ It would take two hours into the conversation before I'd confess that I was crying over you/ She would say "why would you want someone who is married and drinks and does drugs"/ All my life I've been a good child/ My mother survived my father/ I didn't have room to be anything other than *good*/ I never allowed myself to make my own mistakes/

In the first grade, I got separated from the class and the napkin in my lunch blew away/ I was alone at the lunch tables/ Everyone else was eating inside because of the wind, and I'd just lost the note my mother wrote/ I'm a very soft person/ I've been scolded by this world time and time again for being "too sensitive"/ My mother has always been patient with me/ She is the kind of mom who writes notes on school-lunch napkins/ I'm the kind of woman who remembers too much/ It's like I'm trying to hold it all—trying to give it all a meaning/ I often feel like a gust of wind could come and take everything/ I tell my mother, "I know, I know, I know—"/ But you were as soft as me/ *Everything in me knows, everything in me knows.*

What could happen is for the future me to heal from. I can't protect myself from grief or heartbreak,

Unit & Universe

Standing at the canyon edge of this reckoning,
I hold in both hands the sum cups of my life,

I tell Mother Gaia that I've spent all my years
Trying to fill others up—to be seen as *enough*,

Now I kneel to her,
Holding out my empty cups.

I tell her I'm afraid
I don't know the first thing about love.

This mythology, this fallacy,
This paradox of dreams.

I've loved too much and not at all.
There exists in me this struggle between

Everyone has hurt me,
And *I'll never give up my belief.*

I tell her I'm tired of this body,
The gravity it is to be one—

A single unit aging
With every turn of the sun.

I ask her, "What is the meaning of the universe?
What am I?"

The canyons sigh
Like hinges of a door,

But I'm presented with no opening,
Only life's persistent howling.

But the hymns whisper in me:
Isn't it the ebbs and flows of the snow,

The white birch of the tree?
Isn't it aurora borealis, spring's kiss, celestial strings?

Isn't it the yolk of the sun,
That first crack of morning light?

Wasn't it in the flicker of your lover's eyes,
The burst of orgasmic cries?

You're the bloom of goosebumps,
The breath that blows the dandelion,

You're the glimmer of your past lifetimes,
The histories behind the galaxies of your eyes.

My child, there are infinite reasons
Why you came again to be alive,

Inside you is a pilot light,
And it will always keep you

Burning bright—
Your cups flowing ever live.

Loud
I've been calling
out so loud

Is the universe
proud?

Limb & Life

We were the breathlessness
Of running short on legs that soared.

We were twigs of a nest snapping
With each step, crushing robin's eggs.

When all I should have done was ask
Your inner boy to play.

I'll bring the dress-up cape, a mask, and a sword,
So you can be the hero, babe. You'll be the defender

Of the robin's eggs, paint them with bristles blue,
And tuck them in with laundry lint.

You'll make us maps out of leaves,
Wearing boots to your knees or soccer cleats.

I wish to see you so pristine.
Oh and how I will also be:

Collector of ribbons for the swallows
And the doves, my toes in mud,

Carrying baskets of red berry seeds.
I'll even offer a golden hair or three.

We'll be conductors under the sun
And northern skies, prairie grass

And golden daylight, a hundred acres of forest,
A neverland, where the palest speckle blue

Isn't crushed by the evil that the grown do.
You'll protect me like the eggs—your partner

In the most marvelous of games.
But soon will come the day, where I look to you

And see no golden boy of joy, but a tempered
Man of age. You'll turn from me in shame,

The subtle rage flowing in your veins.
In tragedy I'll see, my legs have also raised.

It's only inevitable when your hands
Divide my thighs,

Your body atop of mine.
I'm all woman below you—bare and essential,

Like the soft core of forbidden fruit.
In the red of your gaze my innocence

Will be extinguished—
Our playfulness replaced with bliss

As we cease to see
Beyond our physicality.

When we awake, on the edge of this frontier,
I'll stand and offer you my hand,

But you'll tell me you don't have time
For such senseless play.

You cannot toil in the length of a summer day.
You'll crumple our maps out of leaves

And lose me in a forest of trees.
Now only in nighttime need will you search for me,

When the larks have silenced their songs, and the
Moon has reaped the glow of the day.

You'll whisper across the canopies, and through all
The density I'll hear your somber plea,

You'll appear in front of me,
And through the shadow,

I'll see—who you used to be.
For a moment we'll be golden.

But by the first coos of morning,
You'll forget to be my friend.

The larks will watch us in a lurch
As we lose each other all over again.

Sin by sin you'll hurt me,
Each and every extremity.

The birds will sing in memory,
And when I hear their song,

I'll remember you so pristine—
Cartographer of leaves,

Sure-footed climber of the trees.
As step by step, you go out on a limb.

Turning like a top as you grin
Across the distance.

Your arm extending to mine—*come jump with me!*
Risky and free—our legs go soaring into the breeze.

III: Life

You are an alchemist; make gold of that.
—William Shakespeare

Can We Keep the Dog?

Surely, there is a way we can pause
The sunrise, capture it,
Incarnate the stillness
Of eight in the morning?

We can keep butterflies,
Canopies, and the tallest trees. Perhaps, we can even
Preserve . . . delay—the magic of intimacy.
We can collect coins and folded bills,

To store them safe in our deep-pilled pockets.
We can have cracked candy cemented
On the backs of our baby molar teeth,
To taste the sweetness later.

But the day must come where our molars fall
Away from our pink grinning gums,
Tumbling from our changing lip line
And shifting the nature of our smile.

We must trade our coins and forfeit our bills,
Investing in bigger and better and more.
So much gamble. So much praise.
There must be strategy

And sacrifice and persistence...
But must the integrity of a first kiss elapse into
Something barely feigning romance?
Must we end our quest for that essence, that eternal

Dance, that chased-after flame...?
Is it all a myth that we must extinguish?
Must eight always turn to nine?
Does calm always have to be displaced by time?

See, I fear the surest must of all is that what rises
Always risks a fall. We say good night to the sun...
And when the child begs the question...
We pray that someone else can save the dog.

Can we keep the Day?
Can we keep sunsets
or the eight o'clock
hour

Can we keep innocence
or a belief in intimacy

Can we keep coins
in our pockets or candy
on the backs of our
baby molars for later

or must we scrub out
teeth trade our coins

Must we turn from
first kisses and
abandon our loveliest
beliefs

Must eight inevitably
become nine and
must the sun say
goodbye?

Can We keep the Day?
Can we keep sunsets
or the stillness of
8 a.m.?

Can we keep childhood
butterflies, canopies, and
the tallest trees? can
been apertures can save
of intimacy is the magic

Can we keep coins and
folded bills in our
deep filled pockets the
ones journey by
man? Maybe it would
be better to keep
the sugar caked in
our baby molars in beds
teeth for remnants
of candy gifted to
shiny handed down
from giving hands
to make our
silica ring candy
Not so sweet after all.

Circling

I still shed tears over my father,
More than I want to.
I'm not healed by hindsight.

The time hasn't made anything right.
I'm still spinning,
Afraid my pedals will fall off.

I don't trust my bike, the spikes, the very foundation
Of the ground that meets my feet.
What stops it from giving out?

Bakery box,
Hopscotch,
All the things I've convinced myself I don't want:

Diamonds,
Babies,
And the warmest springs—

I want to believe,
That *it won't happen to you and me,*
But he left me circling.

Survived Him

He tripped on my opening night.
The show must go on even though Dad
Missed the casting call. I'm it. All on my own.

I'll bring myself roses to the show.
Praise my name on the procession page.
His words always fell absent anyway.

His mind was somewhere else.
Anonymous red lipstick
Would always be preferable over

His daughter and a picnic.
I cried in cars and coffee shops
Where I listened to him confuse me.

So thirsty for a sincere apology.
But it was always "you can't blame me,"
Tangled with a hollow "I'm sorry."

He keeps me in a box. As if he always feared
My existence. Maybe he never could have handled
Me. No love for the woman who gave him me.

He told me that love is a roller coaster. "Sometimes
You have to get the first wife out of the way to find
The second." I hope the ride was worth it.

I'm too afraid to try.
I don't want to crash off course,
Fuck some other woman's first husband.

He can no longer go through me—
Or make me his mouthpiece.
I'm done talking.

He took every word from my river and dried me
Clean. Now I'm rebuilding.
My show does not center on him.

I'll play all the parts. I've always had to.
I'll throw my own roses and bow
At how I survived him.

do you dread my
questions?

↳ Oh how I wish
my forgetting was
as easy as yours

↳ my scabs as
firm as super glue.

Proof of Life

Particles reflect off the window shade.
I trace them with my distant eyes.

I marvel at the touchless space dust,
But my insides are stuck.

I'm too closed like this apartment air.
Stagnant with breathing room.

Particles drift by.
I sit and stare.

I'm made inanimate by my own mind.
I'm like a fleck of dust reflected in window blinds.

I'm 4:00 p.m. light,
The fading daytime.

I'm bothered by the banana peel.
The gnats worship at it like it's heaven's syrup.

My skin twitches from the perspiration,
The sheaths of my growing hair.

The follicles, the pores, my apple core.
It's all of me and my beating, spotting body.

I'm captured alive in
The window light,

Like an ultraviolet device
Bearing the truth to my proof of life.

Fractal of Time

She has frostbitten skin,
Patches of iridescence—ice.

She was a sun queen,
A delicate weaver of her dreams.

Now she's a fading sculpture, her once-glowing skin
In rupture. Rapture of her youth.

Silver strands thorn her crown—her golden prism
Catching white lines.

Snowflakes pucker the parchment of her breasts—for
She is as white as a bride,

As creases gather at the bird's foot of her eyes.
She is a fractal of time.

Shelter Sticks

There are bathroom sinks across America.
Potions, bottles, and pills,
To play human.

To make up a face.
To dance in the space of a body so flawed,
So fleshy and sick.

But our bodies—they dance all the same.
The notes penetrate our bones—
Our shelter sticks.

We dance in these homes
And leak from these ducts
And with some struck of luck

We dance straight into remembrance—
Into someone else's shelter sticks,
And if we dance just right,

We fall all apart,
Into matter turned up by a storm.
Our broken homes forged in another's bones.

Our rebuilding robs the song.
We hurt too much in this form.
Our bodies long

To go out to pasture.
To arrive at that meadow of surrender. To know
The full extent of what it means to be tender.

To be nature.
To be brother and kin.
To be lovers.

To rest your dancing bones in the flowers.
To be greeted by the bee.
To be so free from bathroom sinks

That those lovely,
Lovely dancing bones,
They cease to be.

How could you
not love someone's
pinky finger,

everyone is redeemable

Little Golden Girl

Little Golden Girl dances like a fairy
Across the forest floor. There is something sad
About the golden girl. She twirls
Like she's trying to get the trees to dance.
She's all alone so she spends her days playing

Pretend. She gets cold when the forest turns to snow.
She embodies the rays of the sun, but her light is
Dimming. It's vast, so much room to dance.
She wants someone to come and play.
Her forest echoes so empty.

She was forgotten in the dense green trees.
She's too pure for humanity.
The pines protect her.
They are prepping her to be who she's afraid to be.
Little Golden Girl isn't sure she's ready.

But she longs not to be lonely.
An isolated fairy.
She is fiery.
The ancestor trees burn in her deep.
She's generations ready to speak.

Big Brown Bear finds her first.
He watches her play.
He knows she's ready for the next stage.
Little Golden Girl catches his dark eyes,
Spins to him like she's missed him.

Her eternal playmate.
She isn't alone anymore. But she doesn't want
Big Brown Bear to take her away.
She only wants him to stay.
Big Brown Bear feels at ease as he watches her be.

She's precious to him.
But he knows she must leave.
She doesn't even think to climb the trees to safety.
Her eyes twinkle at him like he's magic. She wants to
Rest her rosy apple cheeks on the fur of his belly

Beast. Big Brown Bear knows he can't be idle
Much longer. He waits for her to tire.
She collapses in the snow like an angel.
She fans her arms and grins at him completely.
She only wants him to be happy.

Big Brown Bear moves toward her.
He tells her she's a rib cage of golden gates.
He tells her not to be scared.
He does not hesitate.
Big Brown Bear bites into Little Golden Girl.

Her belly bleeds into the blanket of snow.
The heavens said "No more,
Spirit girl, you're meant for more."
Big Brown Bear buries Little Golden Girl.
He wraps her snuggly,

She'll be warm for her next eternity.
She'll shine in a new life. Soon the little golden girl's
Bones will be dust on the forest floor.
Little Golden Girl finally rests, she is released,
She is nutrients for the trees.

bleeding into
winter snow,
the heavens
said no more
dancing,
spirit girl,
you're meant
for more,
brown bear
burries golden
girl in
snow,

I write sometimes.
To be in touch
with what I
can't hold,
to feel the
weight of me,
and humanity.
The oneness
of words,
it's more
human than
I'll ever
be,

Writing reminds me of my own morality. My bones will return to dust but my words will always be.
The weight of our words is startling

Centrifuge

I'm tempted to spin out with you,
To dissolve the geometry of me
To make room for this heat. You're some sort of
Refugee and I'm a fool who will let you destroy me,
Toy with me? Split me in two, transfuse?

Arc tangent, acrobatic, gymnastics.
That's the twisted way I fell for you.
Finger sin grip on a playground, merry-go-round,
Where I'll spin out.
It's the high of the ride,

The vector,
The conjecture.
My body is spasms of pleasure.
How does one measure?
The fall, the drug of it all?

The splitting of cells and marrow and autonomy.
Where's the moment it's lost?
The division between you and me,
Before we were infused,
Blood cells of muscle memory.

Is it perfect physics or fatal attraction?
The organized chaos of opposites.
Oxymoronic lovers of fatale.
It's empathy on evil like Adam on Eve.
You're a vector to me.

High ferocious velocity with the magnitude
Of divine serendipity. Intervention from the heavens,
Which sent you hurtling toward me, into my orbit,
The merry-go-round, the center of the world
Where the blue of blood rushes.

The thrill of being five again, no inhibitions, kiss,
Mix, transfix. You transformed me
From the deepest blue, now I'm bleeding golden
For how my heart arced for you.
I fell and reconfigured into something entirely new.

I said, don't mess with my soul's trajjeatory

Apple Seed

I fell into the divine through the portal of your eyes.
I transcended all of space and time.

A love like that swallows the whole of you in a beat
And spits you out like a seed.

But I grew to be nothing short of an apple tree.
I grew, even with an axe at my knees.

When I opened my ears—through the rush
Of sweet blossom blood,

When I opened my bones—through the porousness,
Where your memory had taken residence,

When I opened my mouth—through the metal
Of mercury rising,

When I opened my eyes—through the passage
Of all this time—

I'd arrived.

Acknowledgments

To my mother who always believes in me, to my sister who brings me joy, and to my father who taught me how to make things happen—you all are central to who I am; thank you for being my family.

To my extended family—you've all held me up, and I'm so grateful.

To all my friends who have always said they can't wait to read what I write, have been beside me as I evolve into the person I am becoming, and have allowed me to be a part of their evolutions—you all shine so bright in my life.

To Kerri Resnick for designing a cover so close to my heart that I can feel the gold flowing through my veins. Thank you for taking an interest in this little book and making it come to life.

About the Author

Amanda Lauren is a poet and writer. She has been a storyteller since she was a young child. Writing is a craft that she is electrified by. She views words and writing as a sort of vessel into the beyond. She has a love for philosophy, tranquility among busyness, nature, and the metaphysical. She resides in Southern California with her two cats, Moon and June. She can usually be found with a latte in hand, a moleskin journal, and a maddening thought on her mind. *LIMB & LIFE* is her debut collection of poetry.

About the Book

The book *LIMB & LIFE* is a stunningly raw and poignant poetry collection exploring the depths of the speaker's heart through a confessional and lyrical narrative. In three expertly woven parts, *LIMB & LIFE* investigates deeply introspective questions of heartache, self-identity, body, home, and resilience. The title of this collection derives from the expression "to risk life and limb." While often gut-wrenching and evocative through a coming-of-age journey wrought with loss and grief, the collection arrives at an empowering sense of womanhood and a fuller understanding of what it means to take the risks associated with a fully felt life.

CPSIA information can be obtained
at www.ICGtesting.com
Printed in the USA
LVHW101333091022
730228LV00005B/66